Bobby, the Allotment Robin

Joanne Appleby

Published in 2019 by:

Stellar Books
1 Birchdale
St Mary's Road
Bowdon
Cheshire
WA14 2PW

W: www.stellarbooks.co.uk
E: info@stellarbooks.co.uk

ISBN: 978-191-0275276

All illustrations by Katarina Nice
W: www.kitcatcards.co.uk
E: kitcatcards@gmail.com

Book designed and typeset by Joanne Appleby

Printed in the United Kingdom

The author asserts her moral rights to be identified as the author of her work.

This book belongs to:

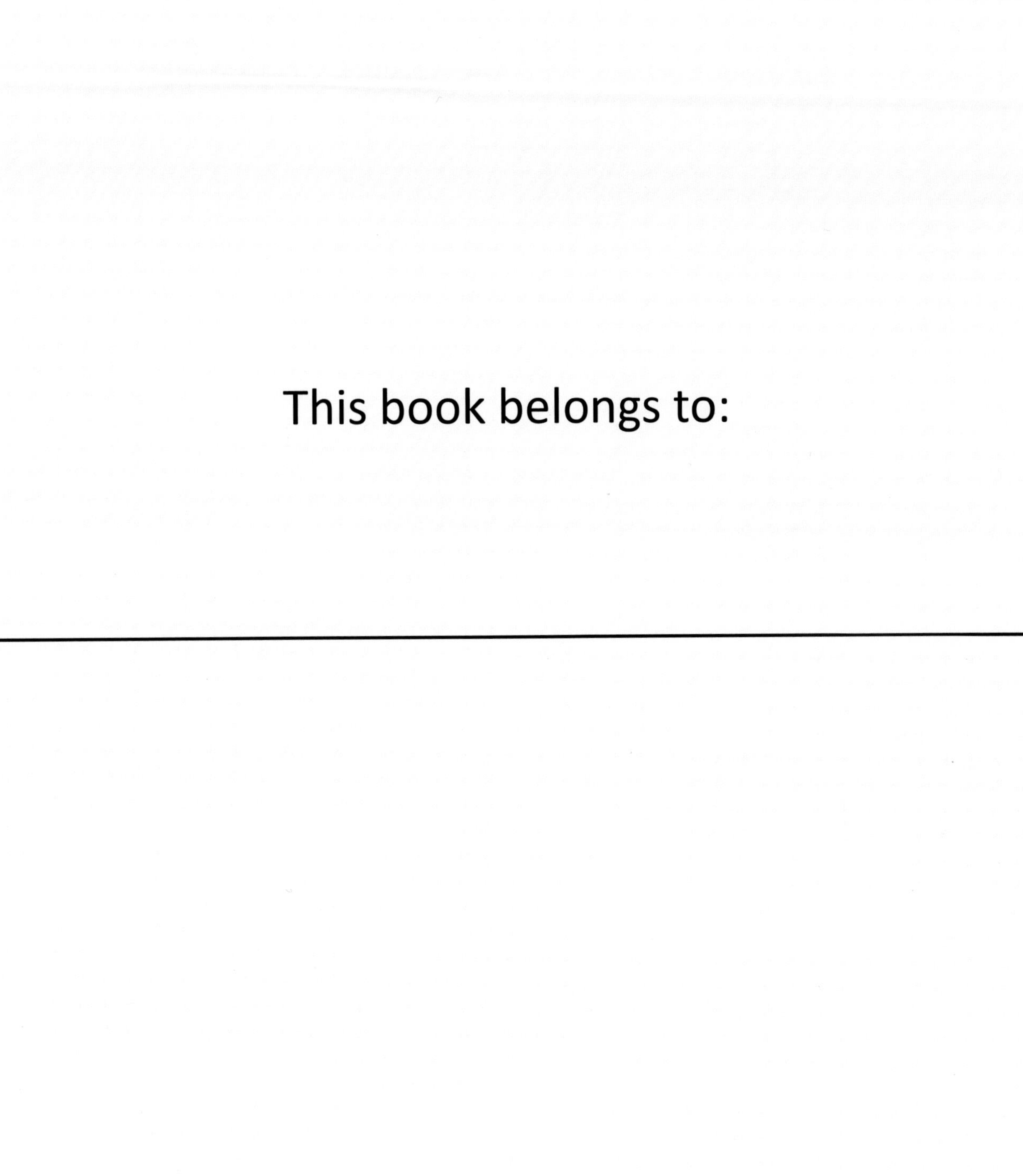

Springtime

Bobby the allotment robin was very excited as spring had arrived and that was when things started to happen in the allotment.

Every spring the Humans came to prepare the allotment and grow their crops.

Bobby Robin was very fond of the two Humans called Gill and Jo, who came to prepare their allotment.

The first task was to clear the weeds and put them on the compost heap.

Bobby liked watching them working hard. He would sit patiently in a tree whilst Gill and Jo dug and weeded the soil.

They raked the soil and made it lovely and smooth.

Bobby would fly down to feast on the juicy worms wriggling over the surface of the smooth soil.

At planting time, Gill planted the seeds very carefully in neat rows:

row 1 potatoes,

row 2 beetroot,

row 3 cabbage,

row 4 broccoli,

row 5 carrots, and

row 6 peas.

Once all the seeds had been planted Gill and Jo put some netting up to stop the greedy wood pigeons and rabbits eating all of the juicy new plants when they first spring up.

Gill and Jo collected water from the water butt and put it into the watering can.

The water butt was full to the top as it had rained a lot over the winter.

The water was used in springtime and summer when it was very dry.

They were careful not to waste a drop of water.

Bobby was very happy as it was time for him to help Scarlet his partner to build a cosy nest for her to lay her eggs, so they could hatch their baby chicks out for the summer.

Bobby collected all the twigs, mud, grass and moss that were needed to build the nest.

Scarlet made the nest nice and snug so she could lay her eggs safely.

Scarlet laid two eggs in the nest.

In just two weeks the chicks would hatch!

Scarlet sat patiently on the eggs in the nest as
Bobby brought her worms.

Summertime

One day when Scarlet was sitting on the nest she felt the eggs move a little!

She hopped off the nest to take a peek.

Oooohhhhhh! Both eggs had started to crack open.

She tweeted for Bobby to fly back to the nest.

Together Bobby and Scarlet watched the eggs hatch.

The two chicks were squeaking as they were very hungry.

Hatching was hard work!

Bobby and Scarlet decided to call their fluffy chicks Poppy and Cherry.

Bobby flew off to find food for the new chicks while Scarlet kept them safe and warm, tucked under her wings.

Bobby flew back to the vegetable patch where Gill and Jo were putting up a bamboo wigwam for the climbing beans.

They put sticks into the soil for the beans to climb up.

Bobby drank from a bowl of water left by Gill and Jo in case he got thirsty.

Bobby flew back to the nest with lots of food for Poppy and Cherry who were very hungry chicks and growing fast too!

Finally it was time for Poppy and Cherry to test their wings to see if they could fly.

Perched on the edge of their nest, they flapped their wings to make sure they were fully warmed up before their very first flight.

All of a sudden Poppy jumped up and took off from the nest.

The chicks were now officially Fledglings and their new home would be a different tree of their choice.

Bobby and Scarlet would keep a watchful eye over them for a little while to make sure they were safe in their big new world.

Now it was time for Poppy and Cherry to make new friends.

Autumn

This was Bobby and Scarlet's favourite time of the year as they loved the juicy blackberries.

They knew they had to feast as much as possible as soon it would be winter and the cold weather meant food would be in short supply.

Bobby and Scarlet watched patiently over Poppy and Cherry as they learnt how to catch worms!

The Humans, Gill and Jo, were picking crops in the allotment.

There was lots of work to do harvesting all of the crops!

The days were getting shorter now and it was starting to get colder at the allotment.

There were frosty cold mornings and not much food to be had for Bobby and Scarlet.

Gill and Jo came to the allotment for the last time before the winter.

Gill and Jo made sure the allotment was tidy and the soil was raked well as it would be a few months before they would return.

They packed the gardening tools away in the shed, making sure they were clean.

Then they took one last look at the allotment.

Bobby and Scarlet watched the Humans as they left the allotment to go home.

They were a little sad as it would be a few months before they would see the Humans again, and it would be a long cold winter with little food.

But they would be excited to see Gill and Jo again in the spring when they would return to start all over again to grow their tasty crops.

Winter

Snow started to fall and Bobby and Scarlet snuggled up together on a tree branch.

They both fell asleep and dreamed of summertime in the allotment when their chicks Poppy and Cherry hatched.

Poppy and Cherry were all snuggled up with their new friends keeping each other nice and warm, dreaming about when they hatched!

Did you know? 5 Facts about Robins

1. The robin is the British National bird, and has been since December 1960.

2. Robins often sing at night.

3. The robin is a member of the thrush family, and so is a relative of the blackbird and the nightingale.

4. A robin's favourite food is mealworms

5. Robins are omnivores, meaning they eat seeds, fruit and insects.